The Power *of*
ATTITUDE

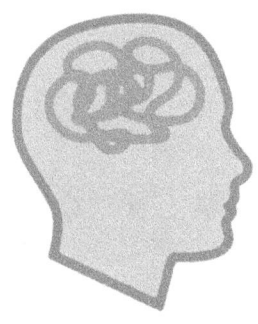

*Devotionals of Wisdom for Living
Life with a Positive, Faith-Filled
Attitude*

RACINE, WI

The Power of Attitude

ISBN: 979-8-88898-174-0 - *Paperback*
ISBN: 979-8-88898-175-7 - *Hardcover*
ISBN: 979-8-88898-176-4 - *Ebook*
Copyright © 2025 by John C. Maxwell & Honor Books, Racine, WI

Cover design and manuscript by Faille Schmitz.

INTRODUCTION

A ttitude . . .
  It is the reflection of our true selves.
  Its roots are inward, but its fruit is outward.
It is our best friend-or our worst enemy.
It is more honest and more consistent than our words.
It is a future outlook based on past experiences.
It draws people to us—or repels them.
It is never content until it is expressed
It is the librarian of our past.
It is the speaker of our present.
It is the prophet of our future.

The quotes and insights in this book have been gleaned from a lifetime of positive thinking and learning. I found out a long time ago that maintaining a positive attitude is the key to personal success in life.

Read, learn, and file these ideas. Then go out and live them, with power!

JOHN C. MAXWELL

WHERE YOU COME ALIVE

There is something sacred about the moment when we stumble upon our purpose. Your heart beats faster, your vision sharpens, and your spirit swells with joy and vigor. Maybe it's when you're helping someone in need, creating something beautiful, negotiating business, or immersed in nature. God designed each of us with a unique fire, a place where our gifts and purpose meet. When we pay attention to where we come alive, we begin to see the shape of the calling God has placed in us.

*The attitude is very important. Because,
your behavior radiates how you feel.*

LOU FERRIGNO

As he thinketh in his heart, so is he.

PROVERBS 23:7

You are only an attitude away from success!

JOHN C. MAXWELL

POWER UP

What makes you come alive?

_____

_____

_____

_____

_____

THE REFINING POWER OF WORK

The highest reward for man's toil is not what he gets for it but what he becomes by it.

JOHN RUSKIN

G old and silver go through a rigorous process of refining to achieve a level of purity prized by all. In a similar way, taking the narrow way through life is not for the faint of heart, but promises great reward. That means not cutting corners, doing the right thing even when it's inconvenient, and pushing through pain. Next time you're knee-deep in the grind, re-member: you're not just getting things done, you're becoming someone stronger, wiser, and more like Christ. That's a reward no paycheck can match.

*It's not whether you get knocked down,
it's whether you get up.*

VINCE LOMBARDI

*. . . the word of the Lord came to Abram in a vision:
"Do not be afraid, Abram. I am your shield, your very
great reward."*

GENESIS 15:1 NIV

*All our dreams can come true—if we have the courage to
pursue them.*

WALT DISNEY

POWER UP

*Reflect on a difficult season in the past that helped shape you
for the better today.*

_____

_____

_____

_____

_____

THE SILVER LINING IN STRUGGLE

In the middle of difficulty lies opportunity.

ALBERT EINSTEIN

It was through severe trial that Joseph in Genesis came into his calling. Rejected and sold into slavery by his own brothers, who would not have been tempted to despair as you were being led away from your homeland in shackles? Yet Joseph keeps his faith and trust in God over the years—even in prison—from where he is finally lifted up out of his struggle and placed in a position of honor and influence for his consistently godly wisdom and conduct. When we lean into difficulty with faith instead of fear, we start to see that it's not a dead end but a setup for something better. Don't rush past the struggle—God is working in it.

*The successful man will profit from his mistakes
and try again in a different way.*

DALE CARNEGIE

*. . . in all these things we are more than conquerors through
him that loved us.*

ROMANS 8:37

*What lies behind us and what lies before us
are tiny matters compared to what lies within us.*

WALT EMERSON

POWER UP

*Let's take a deep dive: what opportunity could be hiding
in your current struggle?*

_____

_____

_____

_____

_____

VISION IN FOCUS

I may not be able to change the world I see around me,
but I can change the way I see the world within me.

The level of injustice, suffering, and chaos being constantly reported in the world can feel overwhelming. There are a million just causes, but how can a single person possibly support or bear the burden of all of them? We might not be able to flip a switch and fix everything around us, but we *can* choose how we see it. That shift in perspective changes everything inside us and enables us to be an effective force for good in your sphere of influence. You can't fix it all, but if every individual resolved to put their hands to what God has before them, it would make a world of difference.

We cannot direct the wind . . . but we can adjust the sails.

CORA L. V. HATCH

The crucible for silver and the furnace for gold,
but people are tested by their praise.

PROVERBS 27:21 NIV

Your attitude determines your action.
Your action determines your accomplishment.

JOHN C. MAXWELL

POWER UP

What is a small action you could take to improve
your sphere of influence?

THE BATTLE OF THE MIND

If you think you are beaten, you are. If you think you dare not, you don't. If you'd like to win but think you can't, it's almost certain you won't.

Our thoughts are powerful. Long before any goal is reached or obstacle overcome, the real fight happens between our ears. If we walk into a challenge already convinced we'll fail, we've handed over the victory before the first step. But when we dare to believe that we can, something shifts. Hope stirs, faith ignites, and courage grows. The truth is, you're stronger than you think, especially when you remember Who has your back.

Your attitude, not your aptitude,
will determine your altitude.

ZIG ZIGLAR

I remain confident of this: I will see the goodness of the Lord
in the land of the living.

PSALM 27:13 NIV

A successful man is one who can lay a firm foundation with
the bricks others have thrown at him.

DAVID BRINKLEY

POWER UP

What is your current mindset producing in your life?

CALM IN THE STORM

If things go wrong, don't go with them.

ROGER BABSON

L ife has a way of throwing curveballs. Unexpected detours, disappointments, or the unraveling of plans can make life feel like a ship rocking in the waves. While the disciples were panicking, imagining their deaths in the middle of a storm in Mark 4, Jesus slept peacefully before they awoke him to calm the storm. This situation seems bizarre at first glance, but there is comfort to be taken in the steadfast peace of Jesus in the midst of chaos. When everything seems to pull you off course, you still have the power to stay rooted in peace, purpose, and truth. Do not let the storm you are in define you — stand your ground on the steady rock of Jesus.

*You are today where your thoughts have brought you;
you will be tomorrow where your thoughts take you.*

JAMES ALLEN

*For what shall it profit a man, if he shall gain
the whole world, and lose his own soul?*

MARK 8:36

*Winning is not everything—
but making the effort to win is.*

VINCE LOMBARDI

POWER UP

*When life takes a downward turn, how you keep yourself
from being swept away by the waves?*

_____

_____

_____

_____

_____

TRUE SUCCESS

---

*You never achieve real success
unless you like what you are doing.*

DALE CARNEGIE

How do you define success? Many would associate material gain and status with success, and to a certain degree the Bible agrees with this. However, the Bible emphasizes that material success is a byproduct of diligent living, not the sole pursuit. When you genuinely enjoy and take ownership of the work set before you, whether it's raising a family, building a business, or serving others in quiet ways, something deeper is at play. That's where real success lives — in the contentment that comes from knowing and fulfilling your purpose on earth with eternity in mind.

You and I do not see things as they are.
We see things as we are.

HERB COHEN

So I commend the enjoyment of life, . . . Then joy will ac-
company them in their toil all the days of the life God has
given them under the sun.

ECCLESIASTES 8:15 NIV

Whether you think you can or think you can't—you are right.

HENRY FORD

POWER UP

How do you find joy in the mundane? What simple glitter of variety
could you add to spark joy in your everyday grind?

DARING TO MOVE FORWARD

I have learned that success is to be measured not so much by the position that one has reached in life as by the obstacles which one has overcome while trying to succeed.

BOOKER T. WASHINGTON

There are points in life where we wrestle through thoughts of self-doubt of our accomplishments and even our purpose. Perhaps you feel you are walking a dark and foggy path, unsure of where your next few footsteps will take you. We cannot know the future, but there are some predictions we can make by looking at our past. How many times have you felt lost, have you weathered a trial, or tripped and fallen only to be rescued and strengthened by God to ultimately overcome? Remember where you've come from, the faithfulness of God in your life, and trust that He will continue to walk with you.

Our attitude toward things is likely to be more important than the things themselves.

A. W. TOZER

These things I have spoken unto you, that in me ye might have peace. In the world ye shall have tribulation: but be of good cheer; I have overcome the world.

JOHN 16:33

Happiness depends not upon things around me, but on my attitude. Everything in my life will depend on my attitude.

ALFRED A. MONTAPERT

POWER UP

Take a moment to look back: what obstacles have you overcome that you never thought you would?

_____

_____

_____

_____

_____

ATTITUDE ADJUSTMENT

The quickest way to correct the other fellow's attitude is to correct your own.

KING VIDOR

Accountability can be a scary word. It is not easy to take a hard look in the mirror, hence why we may feel tempted to point the finger elsewhere. The truth is that we can't control how others respond, but that change begins with us. When we conduct ourselves with humility, patience, and kindness, it shifts the atmosphere. Protect your heart from offense and hypocrisy by focusing on the only attitude you can really control: your own.

Ability is what you're capable of doing. Motivation determines what you do. Attitude determines how well you do it.

LOU HOLTZ

"How can you say to your brother, 'Let me take the speck out of your eye,' when all the time there is a plank in your own eye? You hypocrite, first take the plank out of your own eye, and then you will see clearly to remove the speck from your brother's eye."

MATTHEW 7:4-5 NIV

*God chooses what we go through;
we choose how we go through it.*

JOHN C. MAXWELL

POWER UP

When was the last time you paused to shift your own attitude first, instead of waiting for someone else to change?

THE MIRROR OF OUR HEARTS

It is a fact that you project what you are.

NORMAN VINCENT PEALE

The attitudes, thoughts, and beliefs we carry often show up in the way we treat others. If we're carrying peace, we bring calm. If we're walking in gratitude, we inspire joy. But if our hearts are tangled in bitterness or fear, that can spill out too. The beautiful thing is, with God's help, we can choose what we project. When we draw close to Him, His love, grace, and wisdom begin to shape us from the inside out. When we surrender ourselves to God and allow Him to illuminate the deepest, hidden parts of us with His light, the mirror of our hearts will reflect His goodness.

For I say, through the grace given unto me, to every man that is among you, not to think of himself more highly than he ought to think; but to think soberly, according as God hath dealt to every man the measure of faith.

ROMANS 12:3

Life is not a dress rehearsal.

JOHN C. MAXWELL

A pessimist is a person who, regardless of the present, is disappointed in the future.

POWER UP

What does your heart reflect into the world?

FAITHFUL WITH LITTLE

> *Do not let what you cannot do interfere with what you can do.*
>
> **JOHN WOODEN**

I t's so easy to get hung up on our limitations. We think we must have a certain amount of money, talent, or certain personality traits to achieve our idea of calling. But God doesn't ask us to be perfect or have it all figured out, He just asks us to be faithful with what we *do* have. God called David when he was still a shepherd boy, using a simple rock and sling to conquer Goliath. Don't let what appears out of reach keep you from using what's already in your hands. God does big things with even the smallest offerings.

Since you are my rock and my fortress,
for the sake of your name lead and guide me.

PSALM 31:3 NIV

The greatest day in your life and mine is when we take total
responsibility for our attitudes. That's the day we truly grow
up.

JOHN C. MAXWELL

We cannot continually behave in a manner that is inconsistent
with the way we see ourselves.

POWER UP

What "little" in your life is God calling you to faithfulness in?

MIND SHIFT, LIFE SHIFT

The greatest discovery of our generation is that human beings can alter their lives by altering their state of mind.

WILLIAM JAMES

T he biggest change you can make in your life doesn't start with your circumstances, but with your thoughts. Scripture reminds us to be transformed by the renewing of our minds, because God knows our mindset shapes everything. When we choose to think with gratitude, faith, and hope, we begin to see possibilities where we once saw walls. If you feel stuck today, take heart in the fact that transformation begins with the simple but powerful decision to believe that *change is possible.*

For to be carnally minded is death;
but to be spiritually minded is life and peace.

ROMANS 8:6

The greatest mistake a person can make is doing nothing.

JOHN C. MAXWELL

There is no wrong side of the bed. We get up on the wrong
side of our mind.

POWER UP

What area of your life could be improved by an altering of mindset?

HOPE ON THE HORIZON

> *It is the eye that makes the horizon.*
>
> RALPH WALDO EMERSON

What we see in life often depends on how we choose to look. One person sees dark clouds on the horizon and begrudgingly grabs their umbrella on their way out the door, while another smiles knowing their garden will get a good watering. In 2 Corinthians 4:18, we're encouraged to fix our eyes not on what is seen, but on what is unseen—because the eternal is far more powerful than the temporary. When we look through eyes of faith, hope rises on the horizon.

So we fix our eyes not on what is seen, but on what is unseen, since what is seen is temporary, but what is unseen is eternal.

2 CORINTHIANS 4:18 NIV

Believe you are defeated, believe it long enough, and it is likely to become a fact.

NORMAN VINCENT PEALE

What really matters is what happens in us, not to us.

POWER UP

What do you see on the horizon of your life?

THE BIGGER PICTURE

---

*Every man takes the limits of his own field of vision
for the limits of the world.*

ARTHUR SCHOPENHAUER

This quote is a gentle reminder that our perspective isn't the whole picture. We each carry our own lens shaped by experience, culture, and emotion. In the monotony of life, we can find ourselves with tunnel vision if we aren't careful. But God calls us to see beyond ourselves—to lend our ear to our brothers and sisters, to learn, and to seek His heart. When we ask Him to expand our vision, we better understand the bigger picture of life, can rise above barriers, and are empowered with purpose to live with impact.

"For with God nothing shall be impossible."

LUKE 1:37

Excellence is not a skill, it's an attitude.

RALPH MARSTON

Men may be measured by their reactions to life's inequities.

POWER UP

Where could your field of vision use some expanding?

_____

_____

_____

_____

_____

NATURE VS. NURTURE

*The environment you fashion out of . . . your thoughts
. . . your beliefs . . . your ideals . . . your philosophy . .
. is the only climate you will ever live in.*

ALFRED A. MONTAPERT

T he world outside may shift with every season, but the atmosphere of your life is shaped most deeply by what's going on inside. God invites us to renew our minds daily, to cultivate thoughts that draw us into His love, truth, and promises. When we choose faith instead of fear, gratitude instead of grumbling, and grace instead of judgment, we create a climate where the soul can truly thrive. Your nature is not the main act, only the backdrop. It is within your power to nurture a life of righteousness through Christ Jesus — go forth in faith!

Health, happiness, and prosperity are primarily mental.

MARIAN RAMSAY

You were taught, with regard to your former way of life, to put off your old self, which is being corrupted by its deceitful desires; to be made new in the attitude of your minds . . .

EPHESIANS 4:22-23 NIV

Life is formed from the inside out. What I am inside determines the issues in the battle of life.

DR. WILLIAM HORNADAY

POWER UP

How much of your mindset is a result of your nature? How much is a result of nurture?

THE SECRET TO CONTENTMENT

Very little is needed to make a happy life. It is all within yourself—in your way of thinking and attitude.

FRED CORBETT

We search high and low for happiness, as if it's tucked away in the perfect job, a dream vacation, or someone else's approval. The hard fact is that if you cannot find contentment where you currently stand, the likelihood of happiness being on the other side of your dreams is low. Authentic joy doesn't have to wait for everything to line up just right. It begins with believing that even ordinary days carry extraordinary blessings. With God's help, we can train our hearts to look up, smile more, and find contentment in the here and now.

Man's greatness lies in his power of thought.

BLAISE PASCAL

But godliness with contentment is great gain.

1 TIMOTHY 6:6 NIV

Others can stop you temporarily, but you're the only one who can do it permanently.

JOHN C. MAXWELL

POWER UP

What does achieving contentment look like for you?

GODLY OPTIMISM

The world needs more light-bringers — people who speak hope when things look bleak and encourage others when doubt creeps in. Godly optimism doesn't deny the existence of difficulty, but chooses to believe God's goodness will prevail. If you catch a flicker of hope today, hold it gently in the palm of your hand, nurture it, and share its brilliance with others. You never know who might be standing nearby, needing just a little spark to believe again.

. . . let your light shine before others, that they may see your good deeds and glorify your Father in heaven.

MATTHEW 5:16 NIV

Man must cease attributing his problems to his environment and learn again to exercise his will.

ALBERT SCHWEITZER

Growl all day and you'll feel dog tired at night.

POWER UP

Do you lean towards optimism or pessimism?
How has that shaped your life?

A VICTORY MINDSET

We lost because we told ourselves we lost.

LEO TOLSTOY

O ur inner narrative often shapes our reality. When we speak defeat over ourselves, we tend to shrink, hesitate, and
give up before the breakthrough comes. But what
if we told ourselves the truth instead? That with God,
we are more than conquerors. That we aren't defined
by our failure, but Christ's victory. There are many
circumstances beyond our control, but our outlook
is not one of them.

Blessed is the one who perseveres under trial because, having stood the test, that person will receive the crown of life that the Lord has promised to those who love him.

JAMES 1:12 NIV

Be careful for nothing, prayerful for everything, thankful for anything.

DWIGHT L. MOODY

Never look back unless you want to go that way.

POWER UP

How might your life transform if, instead of telling yourself you might lose, you chose to believe you will win?

WHAT STINK?

If a man has a Limburger cheese on his upper lip,
he thinks the whole world smells.

JOHN C. MAXWELL

Have you ever noticed that when your heart is weighed down with bitterness, frustration, or negativity, the whole world seems to sour? If we're carrying resentment or fear, it's easy to project our issues onto others, but maybe it's time to check our own "upper lip." Ask God to clear your perspective today. A little grace, a little humility, and a little heart-cleansing can suddenly make the world feel a whole lot sweeter.

I go at what I do as if there were nothing else in the world for me to do.

CHARLES KINGSLEY

A merry heart maketh a cheerful countenance: but by sorrow of the heart the spirit is broken.

PROVERBS 15:13

Places and circumstances never guarantee happiness. You must decide within yourself whether you want to be happy.

ROBERT J. HASTINGS

POWER UP

What typically determines your attitude and how does it color your day?

_____

_____

_____

_____

_____

WISDOM IN THE STUMBLE

---

*Failure is only the opportunity
to begin again more intelligently.*

HENRY FORD

E very time we stumble, we gain insight
we didn't have before. The beauty of this
quote reminds us that falling short doesn't
mean we're finished; it means we're now better
equipped to start again with trained eyes. Setbacks
happen and God uses them to teach, shape, and pre-
pare us for what's next. So if something didn't go
the way you hoped, don't get discouraged. Take a
deep breath, learn from it, and step forward with
faith and a little more wisdom than before.

Blessed is the one who perseveres under trial because, having stood the test, that person will receive the crown of life that the Lord has promised to those who love him.

JAMES 1:12 NIV

Action and feeling go together, and by regulating the action, . . . we can directly regulate the feeling.

WILLIAM JAMES

Opportunity looks bigger going than coming.

POWER UP

How do you handle failure?

THE LORD'S WORK

> *The quality of a person's life is in direct proportion to their commitment to excellence, regardless of their chosen field of endeavor.*
>
> VINCE LOMBARDI

What if the secret to a truly fulfilling life isn't about *what* you do, but *how* you do it? This quote gently nudges us to remember that greatness isn't reserved for certain careers or callings, but it's born in the heart of anyone who chooses to give their best. Whether you're teaching in a classroom, raising a family, or stocking shelves, a life committed to excellence has a larger ripple effect than you may realize. God honors the diligence and dedication of His children. Put your heart into the task before you, and your faithfulness will reflect something extraordinary.

Attitude is a little thing that makes a big difference.

WINSTON CHURCHILL

Whatever you do, work at it with all your heart,
as working for the Lord, not for men.

COLOSSIANS 3:23 NIV

Always bear in mind that our own resolution to succeed is
more important than any other one thing.

ABRAHAM LINCOLN

POWER UP

How could you exercise greatness, however simple,
in your current season of life?

_____

_____

_____

_____

_____

THE POWER OF ATTITUDE

> *To live a long time and to enjoy life, the unseen force for you to develop is the proper attitude.*
>
> ALFRED A. MONTAPERT

We manage our health through routines and remedies, but lasting joy and vitality often spring from something far less visible. Stress is linked to a weakened immune system, increased risk for heart disease, and digestive issues. The fuel for a vibrant life isn't found in circumstances, but in the lens through which we view them. A heart and mind rooted in God has the power to transform the struggle and the ordinary into something beautiful. Choose to believe the best, to look for light, and to walk forward with a spirit that lifts — not just your years — but the life in them.

*The quality of an individual is reflected in the standards
they set for themselves.*

RAY KROC

*Commit thy way unto the Lord; trust also in him;
and he shall bring it to pass.*

PSALM 37:5

*The purpose of human life is to serve,
and to show compassion and the will to help others.*

ALBERT SCHWEITZER

POWER UP

*Take a moment for faith-filled imagination:
what does God's best look like in the next year of your life?*

_____

_____

_____

_____

_____

THOUGHT LIFE - REAL LIFE

> *The man who acquires the ability to take full possession of his own mind may take possession of anything else to which he is justly entitled.*
>
> ANDREW CARNEGIE

There's incredible power in learning to curate your own thoughts. When we anchor our thinking in the truth of the Word and invite the Holy Spirit into our thought life, we begin to walk with clarity, confidence, and courage. We all have passing thoughts in our minds that we aren't proud of, but they do not define us. Take every thought captive, give it to God, and watch how your inner life begins to thrive and overflow into the world around you.

Who is rich? He that rejoices in his portion.

BENJAMIN FRANKLIN

And we know that all things work together for good to them that love God, to them who are the called according to his purpose.

ROMANS 8:28

Nothing is as hard as it looks; everything is more rewarding than you expect; and if anything can go right it will and at the best possible moment.

MAXWELL'S LAW

POWER UP

How could you grow in the skill of curating your thoughts?

THE CARPENTER'S CHISEL

I thank God for my handicaps, for through them I have found myself, my work, and my God.

HELEN KELLER

Sometimes the very things we wish we could change about ourselves become the very things God uses to shape us. This quote invites us to see our struggles as sacred tools of discovery. When life forces us to face our limits, it is an invitation to reach out to our Father for strength. In our weakness, His strength is revealed. Don't despise the valleys in your story — they may be the chisel God is using to carve something beautiful and eternal.

There is no security in this life, only opportunity.

GENERAL DOUGLAS MACARTHUR

My flesh and my heart faileth: but God is the strength of my heart, and my portion for ever.

PSALM 73:26

Where there is no hope in the future, there is no power in the present.

JOHN C. MAXWELL

POWER UP

What is God chiseling in your life right now?

FREEDOM FROM IMPRESSION

> *Success is peace of mind in knowing you did your best.*
>
> JOHN WOODEN

Here is a gentle reminder that real success isn't found in applause, but in inner peace. When you've shown up with integrity, poured in your effort, and stayed true to your values, that's something to celebrate whether or not anyone else notices. God doesn't ask for perfection; He asks for *faithfulness*. So today, take a deep breath and let go of the pressure to impress. If you've done your best, you've already succeeded in the only way that truly matters. Isn't that a freeing thought?

Anyone who stops learning is old, whether at twenty or eighty. Anyone who keeps learning stays young.

HENRY FORD

Whatever you do, work at it with all your heart, as working for the Lord, not for human masters, since you know that you will receive an inheritance from the Lord as a reward. It is the Lord Christ you are serving.

COLOSSIANS 3:23-24 NIV

Football games are generally won by the boys with the greatest desire.

PAUL "BEAR" BRYANT

POWER UP

What is your "best" in this season of life?

THE BEAT OF YOUR DRUM

> *The attitude of the individual determines the attitude of the group.*
>
> JOHN C. MAXWELL

Attitude is powerfully contagious. As early as the 16th century, musicians were present in the ranks of soldiers on the battlefield. What might seem a frivolous idea in our modern outlook on war set rhythm, boosted morale, and fostered unity among men charging into battle together. Our attitudes often come through in our tone, and the tone of our voices and actions can skew their effect, for better or for worse. Let the beat of your drum inspire encouragement in those around you today.

If a man has done his best, what else is there?

GENERAL GEORGE S. PATTON

Beloved, let us love one another: for love is of God; and every one that loveth is born of God, and knoweth God.

1 JOHN 4:7

The last of the human freedoms is to choose one's attitude in any given set of circumstances.

VICTOR FRANKL,
SURVIVOR OF NAZI CONCENTRATION CAMP

POWER UP

What is the beat of your drum?

CONFIDENCE IS KEY

> *It is no exaggeration to say that a strong, positive self-image is the best possible preparation for success in life.*
>
> DR. JOYCE BROTHERS

The way you see yourself shapes the way you move through the world. If you believe you're capable, loved, and created with purpose, you'll walk into each challenge with quiet confidence. God calls you His masterpiece (Ephesians 2:10), not because you're flawless, but because you're His. A positive self-image doesn't come from perfection or comparison, but from embracing who you are in Christ. Speak to yourself today with the kindness and truth you'd offer a friend.

Watch your life and doctrine closely. Persevere in them, be-cause if you do, you will save both yourself and your hearers.

1 TIMOTHY 4:16 NIV

I expect the best and with God's help will attain the best.

NORMAN VINCENT PEALE

Misery is an option!

POWER UP

What is the current state of your self-image? What are some steps you could take to improve?

_____

_____

_____

_____

_____

NO RECORD OF WRONGS

*You never get ahead of anyone
as long as you try to get even with them.*

Trying to get even might feel satisfying in the moment, but it keeps you stuck in the same cycle as the person who hurt you. True growth comes when you rise above, not out of vengeance, but out of authenticity. God calls us to forgive not just for their sake, but for ours. When we release resentment, we make space for joy, healing, and forward motion. So instead of matching someone's wrong, match God's grace. You'll find yourself moving forward lighter and happier without the weight of bitterness.

If you love those who love you, what reward will you get? Are not even the tax collectors doing that? And if you greet only your own people, what are you doing more than others? Do not even pagans do that?

MATTHEW 5:46-47 NIV

I firmly believe that any man's finest hour—his greatest fulfillment to all he holds dear—is that moment when he has worked his heart out in a good cause and lies exhausted on the field of battle—victorious.

VINCE LOMBARDI

Maintain the right attitude is easier than regaining the right attitude.

POWER UP

Do you have any resentment or unforgiveness in your life that is robbing you of joy?

SLOW AND STEADY

Don't let yourself . . .
Worry when you're doing your best.
Hurry when success depends on accuracy.
Think evil of anyone until you have the facts.
Believe a thing is impossible without trying it.

L ife moves fast. Our culture is obsessed with the quickest return on our investments, but wisdom is the steady compass that keeps us on track. God invites us to walk wisely, trust completely, work diligently, and act boldly. Don't get swept up in the rat race. Take one step at a time, with grace and courage, and you'll go further than you imagined.

Aim for the highest.

ANDREW CARNEGIE

*From the fruit of their lips people are filled with good things,
and the work of their hands brings them reward.*

PROVERBS 12:14 NIV

*Even a mistake may turn out to be the one thing necessary
to a worthwhile achievement.*

HENRY FORD

POWER UP

*Are you content to take things slow,
or do you find yourself rushing for results?*

YOU ARE WHO YOU THINK

Our greatest tool for growth isn't luck, talent, or timing—it's our *mindset*. A person with the right attitude sees obstacles as stepping stones and setbacks as setups for something better. With faith and focus, no goal is out of reach. But even the most gifted person can be rendered ineffective by their outlook. Nurture a mentally and spiritually healthy attitude with consistent time in God's word, because how we think shapes how we live.

Now the God of patience and consolation grant you to be likeminded one toward another according to Christ Jesus . . .

ROMANS 15:5

Life is like baseball; it's 95% mental and the other half is physical.

YOGI BERRA

I'm not sure all happy people are generous, but I've never seen a generous person who isn't happy.

POWER UP

Is your current attitude building a pathway toward your goals, or is it an obstacle?

SMALL BEGINNINGS

If you want to change attitudes, start with a change in behavior. In other words, begin to act the part, as well as you can, of the person you would rather be, the person you most want to become. Gradually, the old, fearful person will fade away.

DR. WILLIAM GLASSER

The biggest transformations start with the first small step. If you long to be more confident, kind, or courageous, don't wait to feel ready — start *acting* ready. Show up as the person you want to grow into, and over time, your actions will shape your identity. As you practice faith, bravery, or grace, old fears lose their grip as they are replaced by the truth of who you're becoming. God isn't waiting for perfection, He's patiently waiting for you invitation to partner with you in your progress.

Lazy hands make for poverty, but diligent hands bring wealth.

PROVERBS 10:4 NIV

For success, attitude is equally as important as ability.

WALTER SCOTT

Attitudes determine actions. You are not what you think you are. What you think, you are!

POWER UP

What is holding you back from taking the first step towards a goal or dream?

_____

_____

_____

_____

_____

CHALLENGE AS OPPORTUNITY

Accept the challenges so that you may feel the exhilaration of victory.

GENERAL GEORGE S. PATTON

Every mountain we face holds not just struggle, but also great opportunity for reward, growth, and fulfillment. Victory isn't found by lingering in the comfort zone, but it waits beyond in unexplored territory. When we say yes to difficulty instead of retreating from it, we give ourselves the chance to witness God's strength in us. The comfort of safety is but of sliver of the joy of taking God's hand and letting Him guide you through challenge to victory.

The Lord is my portion, saith my soul;
therefore will I hope in him.

LAMENTATIONS 3:24

Every man over forty is responsible for
[the disposition of] his face.

ABRAHAM LINCOLN

People catch our spirit just like they catch our colds—
by getting close to us.

POWER UP

When was the last time you truly challenged yourself?

CHOOSING JOY

A happy person is not a person in a certain set of circumstances, but rather a person with a certain set of attitudes.

HUGH DOWNS

The world would have you believe that happiness is found in accomplishment, in wealth, in romance, or in status. While these things can certainly add to life, they are not guaranteed keys to happiness. A miserable person alone in a studio apartment simply finds more room and company to be miserable with in a mansion. Some of the happiest people are those who have chosen to see goodness even in the midst of lack or difficulty. When we align ourselves with God's truth, we begin to see joy not as a goal, but as a steady companion.

Do not conform to the pattern of this world, but be transformed by the renewing of your mind. Then you will be able to test and approve what God's will is—his good, pleasing and perfect will.

ROMANS 12:2 NIV

Keep your face to the sunshine and you cannot see the shadows.

HELEN KELLER

Instead of saying TGIF, say TGIT—Thank God it's today!

POWER UP

Are you waiting for your circumstances to change in order to be happy? Consider what simply joys you may be taking for granted.

_____

_____

_____

_____

_____

TECHNICOLOR LIFE

Afflictions color your life, but you choose the color.

To be human on this side of eternity is to endure some degree of hardship. Jesus promises us this in John 16, but it comes with a message of hope: *"I have told you these things, so that in me you may have peace. In this world you will have trouble. But take heart! I have overcome the world."* Paint is messy, not unlike life. The picture of your life may not be perfect, but in His hands, it is a masterpiece. Collaborate with God today in the daily brushstrokes of your life.

Sales are not made or unmade inside the prospect's office. They are made or unmade inside you.

BRIAN AZAR

. . . we also glory in our sufferings, because we know that suffering produces perseverance; perseverance, character; and character, hope. And hope does not put us to shame, because God's love has been poured out into our hearts through the Holy Spirit, who has been given to us.

ROMANS 5:3-5 NIV

People don't care how much you know until they know how much you care.

JOHN C. MAXWELL

POWER UP

If your life was a painting, what would it look like?

DIG DEEP

Wars may be fought with weapons, but they are won by men. It is the spirit of the men who follow and of the man who leads that gains victory.

GENERAL GEORGE S. PATTON

A t the peak of battle, when you're beginning to grow weary, it's your spirit that carries you through to victory. While strength and resources matter, it is courage, integrity, hope, and conviction that God uses to extend us beyond our natural ability. The leader who inspires with purpose, and the follower who believes with heart, create a force to be reckoned with. So when the fight feels long, dig deep within yourself and tap into the well of strength that comes from Christ in you.

Iron sharpeneth iron; so a man sharpeneth the countenance of his friend.

PROVERBS 27:17

Well done is better than well said.

BENJAMIN FRANKLIN

It is unfortunate when people allow themselves to get like concrete—all mixed up and permanently set.

POWER UP

When you are weary, what gives you that last bit of strength to push through?

SUCCESS MINDSET

Success or failure in business is caused more by the mental attitude than by mental capacities.

I n God's economy, success isn't just about skill, but the heart you bring to the work. You can have all the talent in the world, but if you approach your calling with fear, doubt, or negativity, you'll find the road harder than it needs to be. On the other hand, even modest abilities, when paired with a diligent, faith-filled attitude, can open doors you never imagined. Scripture reminds us, "*As a man thinks in his heart, so is he*" (Proverbs 23:7). So guard your thoughts and trust that with a pure heart, God can turn ordinary effort into extraordinary impact.

We cannot change our past. We cannot change the fact that people act in a certain way. We cannot change the inevitable. The only thing we can do is play on the one string we have, and that is our attitude.

CHARLES R. SWINDOLL

Finally, brothers and sisters, whatever is true, whatever is noble, whatever is right, whatever is pure, whatever is lovely, whatever is admirable—if anything is excellent or praiseworthy—think about such things.

PHILIPPIANS 4:8 NIV

Your attitude is the outward expression of an inward feeling.

JOHN C. MAXWELL

POWER UP

What testimony does your current attitude at your workplace give to those around you?

THE ADVENTURE OF FAITH

Life is either a daring adventure or nothing.

HELEN KELLER

L ife with God was never meant to be lived in safe little boxes. It's a daring, unfolding journey that calls us to trust Him beyond what we can see. All throughout scripture we see God call regular people to extraordinary callings, often not because of their achievements or prowess, but because they had willing hearts. Faith invites us to step out of the boat and to see challenges not as threats, but as opportunities to witness God show up in a powerful way. Don't let life pass you by—take a daring step towards God and He will not disappoint.

He that tilleth his land shall have plenty of bread: but he that followeth after vain persons shall have poverty enough.

PROVERBS 28:19

A positive attitude causes a chain reaction of positive thoughts, events and outcomes. It is a catalyst and it sparks extraordinary results.

WADE BOGGS

Man creates his environment—mental, emotional, and physical —by the attitude he develops.

POWER UP

Do you prefer to live within your comfort zone, or are you willing to embrace life as the adventure God created it to be?

WORK: OUR WITNESS

A good work ethic has always been a prized trait, but it's become a rare one. Whether it's out of demoralization or genuine laziness, it has become the norm to perform at the bare minimum or less at work. The Bible is full of teaching and wisdom exhorting Christians to stand out as excellent workers. Jesus Himself taught that if someone asks you to go one mile, go two. That second mile is where character is forged, blessings overflow, and God's light is most visible in us. When we choose to exceed what's required, we step out of mediocrity and transform our work into our witness.

The wise store up choice food and olive oil,
but fools gulp theirs down.

PROVERBS 21:20 NIV

Every change in human attitude must come through internal understanding and acceptance. Man is the only known creature who can reshape and remold himself by altering his attitude.

JOHN C. MAXWELL

We are either the masters or the victims of our attitudes. It is a matter of personal choice—blessing or curse.

POWER UP

Do you challenge yourself to go above and beyond or are you content doing the bare minimum?

BUILDING OVER BLAMING

During His ministry, Jesus rebuked sin and convicted hearts, but He also offered hope, healing, and ultimately salvation. Jesus saw the problem and ushered in the remedy: the perfect and final sacrifice for all sin. He calls us to be peacemakers and healers, people who bring light where there is darkness. When we approach problems with a redemptive mentality, we mirror Christ's own heart. He never left us in our faults, but became the remedy Himself.

And whosoever of you will be the chiefest,
shall be servant of all.

MARK 10:44

Every problem has in it the seeds of its own solution.
If you don't have any problems, you don't get any seeds.

NORMAN VINCENT PEALE

A positive mental attitude is rooted in clear, calm, and honest
self-confidence.

POWER UP

When you encounter a problem, do you get swallowed up in it or are
you able to move towards a resolution?

_____

_____

_____

_____

_____

INNER CALM IN THE STORM

The situation you live in doesn't have to live in you.

ROBERTA FLACK

L ife can sometimes place us in hard, messy, or uncertain situations, but the good news is we don't have to let those circumstances define us. This quote reminds us that while storms may rage around us, we can still carry calm within. God gives us the ability to guard our hearts and keep our spirits anchored in Him, no matter what is happening externally. When we choose to fill our inner world with gratitude, peace, and trust, we carry a fire that no outside darkness can put out.

Set your minds on things above, not on earthly things.

COLOSSIANS 3:2 NIV

You are where you are and why you are because of the dominating thoughts that occupy your mind.

JOHN C. MAXWELL

Do you see the green near every sand trap, or the sand traps around every green?

POWER UP

How do difficult circumstances color your life? Are you able to rise above or do they define you?

_____

_____

_____

_____

_____

THE ART OF POSITIVITY

> *The good news is that the bad news can be turned into good news when you change your attitude.*
>
> ROBERT SCHULLER

D ark clouds come — loved ones pass, money gets tight, and work gets hard, but rainbows only form with some rain. A setback can either feel like the end of the road or the beginning of a something new. It all depends on the lens we use. With faith, hope, and a willing heart, God can take what looks like devastation and reshape it into opportunity, strength, or even blessing. Sometimes the very thing we dread can become a catalyst for something better than we ever imagined.

And we know that all things work together for good to them that love God, to them who are the called according to his purpose.

ROMANS 8:28

Attitude is the criterion for success. But you can't buy an attitude for a million dollars. Attitudes are not for sale.

DENIS WAITLEY

Our children are like mirrors—they reflect our attitudes in life.

POWER UP

What situation in your life could be transformed with a positive attitude?

_____

_____

_____

_____

_____

FAITH IN ACTION

> *Man who say it cannot be done should not interrupt the man doing it.*
>
> **CHINESE PROVERB**

There will always be voices that say *"it can't be done"*, but those voices don't hold the pen that writes your story. When God plants a dream in your heart, it isn't for everyone else to understand—it's for you to live out. Critics may watch from the sidelines, but great victory belongs to the ones who step forward in faith and keep going. So keep building, keep believing, and let your perseverance be the loudest response to doubt.

In the same way, faith by itself, if it is not accompanied by action, is dead.

JAMES 2:17 NIV

The higher you go in any organization of value, the better the attitude you'll find.

JOHN C. MAXWELL

Beware of those who stand aloof and greet each venture with reproof; the world would stop if things were run by men who say, "It can't be done."

POWER UP

What step haven't you taken because you doubt your success?

CHILDLIKE FAITH

Youth is meant to be filled with dreams, energy, and the excitement of possibility. Jesus treasured the uninhibited faith of children, saying unless you have comparable faith that you would never enter the kingdom of heaven. When we trade that for cynicism and sophistication, we miss the beauty of what God can do in and through us. Choose to see the world through eyes of faith and wonder, trusting that your unknown future will be met by a faithful God.

But the Lord said to Samuel, "Do not consider his appearance or his height, for I have rejected him. The Lord does not look at the things people look at. People look at the outward appearance, but the Lord looks at the heart."

1 SAMUEL 16:7 NIV

We are confronted with insurmountable opportunities.

WALT KELLEY

Never accept the negative until you have thoroughly explored the positive.

POWER UP

How could you foster a child-like imagination and faith in your life?

INNER WORK, OUTER EVIDENCE

> *A person cannot travel within*
> *and stand still without.*
>
> **JAMES ALLEN**

Inner growth will always reveal itself outwardly. When we allow God to transform our hearts by shaping our thoughts, refining our character, and deepening our faith, it naturally flows into how we live and speak. Don't be discouraged if the changes feel small or if they aren't translating outwardly yet. A fruitful tree is the result of years of roots digging deep for nutrients, branches reaching for the sky, and leaves converting sunlight into energy—*it doesn't happen overnight*. Every step forward within is a step toward a fruitful life.

Nothing will be attempted if all possible obstacles must first be removed.

SAMUEL JOHNSON

At least there is hope for a tree: If it is cut down, it will sprout again, and its new shoots will not fail.

JOB 14:7 NIV

My great concern is not whether you have failed, but whether you are content with your failures.

ABRAHAM LINCOLN

POWER UP

What inner work are you currently investing in, and what return are you betting on?

THINKING BIG

> *When you affirm big, believe big, and pray big, big things happen.*
>
> **NORMAN VINCENT PEALE**

Many of us have known that tug of war between faith and humility in our prayer requests. We desire God's will to be done and surrender our situations to Him with open-ended prayers, but don't often get specific or scale our human-sized problems with God-sized results. James 4 convicts us with one statement: *"You do not have because you do not ask God."* Make that desire of your heart known to your Father today, no matter how impossible it may seem. Making the impossible possible is God's specialty.

Jesus replied, "Truly I tell you, if you have faith and do not doubt, not only can you do what was done to the fig tree, but also you can say to this mountain, 'Go, throw yourself into the sea,' and it will be done.

MATTHEW 21:21 NIV

Failure isn't failure unless you don't learn from it.

DR. RONALD NIEDNAGEL

We cannot tailor make the situations of our life, but we can tailor make the attitudes to fit them before they arrive.

POWER UP

What big things are you believing and praying for?

LEARNING FROM DEFEAT

> *Every success I know has been reached because the person was able to analyze defeat and actually profit from it in the next undertaking.*
>
> WILLIAM MARSTON

Every failure carries a lesson, every disappointment holds a seed of wisdom, and every stumble can strengthen the next step if we let it. When we suffer defeat, we have the power to turn it around into new growth. Romans 5 encourages us for just these times: *"suffering produces perseverance; perseverance, character; and character, hope."* Instead of fearing failure, we can welcome it as part of the process that shapes us into stronger, wiser, and more empathetic people.

Laughter is the shortest distance between two people.

VICTOR BORGE

The fear of the Lord is the beginning of knowledge: but fools despise wisdom and instruction.

PROVERBS 1:7

If you have a will to win, you have achieved half your success; if you don't, you have achieved half your failure.

DAVID AMBROSE

POWER UP

What personal defeat has made you wiser?

SUCCEEDING TOGETHER

> *You can get everything in life you want if you help enough other people get what they want.*
>
> ZIG ZIGLAR

When we shift our focus from self-centered striving to lifting others up, true success if found. Doors open, relationships deepen, and blessings multiply in unexpected ways. All throughout Jesus's ministry, we see Him consistently investing in people He met along the way—healing, convicting, and teaching with the utmost humility. God designed us to thrive in community, where generosity, encouragement, and compassion create ripple effects that always circle back. The more we pour into others, the more fulfilled and joyful our own lives become.

And whosoever shall exalt himself shall be abased; and he that shall humble himself shall be exalted.

MATTHEW 23:12

Circumstances do not make you what you are . . . they reveal what you are!

JOHN C. MAXWELL

Life is ten percent how we make it; ninety percent how we take it.

POWER UP

Who was the last person you helped achieve a goal? Who was the last person who aided you in achieving a goal?

NO EXCUSES

Accountability is uncomfortable. It goes against our human nature to highlight something we've done wrong. Excuses may help avoid discomfort in the moment, but they keep us stuck, robbing us of growth, progress, and the joy of accomplishment. God gives us strength and wisdom for every step, but we must choose to rise, act, and keep moving forward—even when it's hard. When we stop justifying why we can't and start trusting that with Him we can, we trade excuses for empowerment and failure for victory.

Each one should test their own actions.

GALATIANS 6:4 NIV

Adopting the right attitude can convert a negative stress into a positive one.

HANS SELYE

If a man be gracious and courteous to strangers, it shows he is a citizen of the world.

POWER UP

Are you making any excuses in your life now that may be delaying breakthrough?

TRUE WISDOM

It is what you learn after you know it all that counts.

JOHN WOODEN

Many of us work our whole lives to achieve a desired level of success and comfort in life. Once you *"arrive"*, the energy that drove you can stagnate into pride and emptiness. Godly wisdom is found in humility, and placing our deepest values in the eternal over the material. God blesses the heart that is willing to keep learning, even in unexpected places and from unexpected people. When we remain teachable, we find that life never stops offering treasures of insight and opportunities for growth.

*Lord, grant that I may always desire more
than I can accomplish.*

MICHELANGELO

*Where is the wise person? Where is the teacher of the law?
Where is the philosopher of this age? Has not God made
foolish the wisdom of the world?*

1 CORINTHIANS 1:20 NIV

*Again and again, the impossible problem is solved when we
see that the problem is only a tough decision waiting to be
made.*

ROBERT SCHULLER

POWER UP

*What wisdom has the past year brought you?
What wisdom do you hope to gain in the next year?*

POWER IN DOING

---

*You're more likely to act yourself into feeling,
than feel yourself into action.*

JEROME BRUNER

Balancing emotion in a healthy way can be incredibly difficult. Giving too much power to your feelings can make life a roller coaster of highs and lows, leading to instability, unnecessary suffering, and a hedonistic lifestyle devoid of order. We often wait until we *"feel like it"* before we move forward, but God calls us to walk by faith with diligence and hard work. Don't wait for the perfect mood to begin; take the first step, and let God shape your feelings through action.

Always help people increase their own self-esteem. Develop your skill in making other people feel important.

DONALD LAIRD

Do not merely listen to the word, and so deceive yourselves. Do what it says.

JAMES 1:22 NIV

Many intelligent people never move beyond the boundaries of their self-imposed limitations.

JOHN C. MAXWELL

POWER UP

What step have you been delaying until it "felt right"?

RESPONSE OVER CIRCUMSTANCE

Events are less important than our responses to them.

JOHN HERSEY

Life is entirely predictable in that is it unpredictable. Inevitably hard times come beyond our control, but we always have control over our response. With God's help, even painful or frustrating circumstances can be met with patience, grace, and resilience. Instead of letting events weigh you down, choose to rise above them by responding in ways that reflect faith, strength, and hope. A godly response can turn trials into testimonies and setbacks into stepping stones.

He hath shewed thee, O man, what is good; and what doth the Lord require of thee, but to do justly, and to love mercy, and to walk humbly with thy God?

MICAH 6:8

I got a simple rule about everybody. If you don't treat me right—shame on you!

LOUIS ARMSTRONG

When opportunity knocks, a grumbler complains about the notice.

POWER UP

How can you choose a response today that reflects faith, strength, and hope rather than simply reacting to your circumstances?

CELEBRATING STRENGTH

God has placed unique gifts and talents within each of us, and sometimes those gifts shine brighter in others than they do in ourselves. Instead of letting pride or jealousy get in the way, we're called to celebrate and work alongside those whose strengths complement our own. When we honor the gifts around us instead of resisting them, we not only build stronger relationships but also serve the ultimate goal of a untied Body of Christ.

Finally, brothers and sisters, rejoice! Strive for full restoration, encourage one another, be of one mind, live in peace. And the God of love and peace will be with you.

2 CORINTHIANS 13:11 NIV

Always make others feel needed, important, and appreciated and they'll return the same to you.

JOHN C. MAXWELL

Your attitude speaks so loudly that I can't hear what you say.

POWER UP

How do the strengths of those around you complement your own?

MAGNIFYING THE POSSIBILITIES

> *A pessimist is one who makes difficulties of his opportunities; an optimist is one who makes opportunities of his difficulties.*
>
> REGINALD B. MANSELL

L ife is full of crossroads where we can either see a wall or a doorway. The pessimist sees rejection and denial in a wall and grumbles, while the optimist looks for a foothold and begins to scale it. The choice is ours: will we magnify the problem or magnify the possibility? When we trust God, every difficulty becomes fertile ground for growth, resilience, and a testimony of His power in our lives.

But Jesus beheld them, and said unto them, "With men this is impossible; but with God all things are possible."

MATTHEW 19:26

When one door closes, another opens; but we often look so long and so regretfully upon the closed door that we do not see the one which has opened for us.

ALEXANDER GRAHAM BELL

Optimism is the cheerful frame of mind that enables a teakettle to sing, though in hot water up to its nose.

POWER UP

When challenges arise, do you focus on the obstacles in your way or might they carry hidden opportunities from God?

FAITH AROUND THE CORNER

An optimist is a driver who thinks that empty space at the curb won't have a hydrant beside it.

CHANGING TIMES

Optimism is not about ignoring reality, but about choosing to expect the best even in uncertain situations. Like the driver, the optimist moves forward with faith instead of fear. Scripture tells us that faith is the assurance of things hoped for (Hebrews 11:1), and that kind of hope is what carries us through life's unknowns. We may not always know what awaits us around the corner, but when we trust in God's goodness, we can step out with confidence. Even if the "hydrant" is there, He will provide another space meant just for us.

If you do what is right, will you not be accepted? But if you do not do what is right, sin is crouching at your door; it desires to have you, but you must rule over it."

GENESIS 4:7 NIV

*Some people look at things as they are and say, "Why?"
I look at things as they can be and say, "Why not?"*

ROBERT KENNEDY

Think right, act right; it is what you think and do that makes you what you are.

POWER UP

Does life around the corner hold hopeful expectation for you or anxiety?

_____

_____

_____

_____

_____

LIVING BOLDLY

Fear of making mistakes can paralyze us more than the mistakes themselves ever could. When we walk in fear, we miss out on opportunities for growth, learning, and even joy. As 2 Timothy 1:7 reminds us, *"For God has not given us a spirit of fear, but of power and of love and of a sound mind."* Mistakes are not final, but are lessons that shape us into wiser people. Step forward boldly today, trusting that even if you stumble, God's hand is steady and His grace is more than enough to lift you back up.

Unless you try to do something beyond what you have already mastered, you will never grow.

RONALD E. OSBORN

*The wicked flee though no one pursues,
but the righteous are as bold as a lion.*

PROVERBS 28:1 NIV

Your problem is not your problem. Your attitude—how you handle your problem—is your problem.

JOHN C. MAXWELL

POWER UP

Think back—what mistake have you made in the past that proved a valuable teaching moment?

THE SELFLESS LIFE

Lasting joy is found not in what we gain, but in what we give. When we bless someone who cannot repay us, we imitate the heart of Jesus, who gave us everything we will never deserve with His sacrifice. These quiet, selfless acts ripple farther than we can see, lighting up the world with God's love in ways we may never know. Each time you give without looking for public recognition, you store up treasures in heaven and experience the deep joy that comes only from serving others. Today, seek a simple way to pour love into someone's life *for the joy of it.*

We all have possibilities we don't know about. We can do things we don't even dream we can do.

DALE CARNEGIE

I know that there is nothing better for people than to be happy and to do good while they live.

ECCLESIASTES 3:12 NIV

Each day we need good thoughts to live by. And remember . . . you get what you order in life.

ALFRED A. MONTAPERT

POWER UP

Is there anyone in your life that could use a hand? Make a plan to pour out love and care into someone with no expectation for repayment.

BE A LIFELONG LEARNER

> *Take the attitude of a student, never be too big to ask questions, never know too much to learn something new.*
>
> OG MANDINO

Life is God's classroom, and every day brings new lessons if we keep the humility of a student. When we think we know it all, our hearts close to growth. When we stay curious and teachable, God can shape us into something greater. Even Jesus' disciples had to keep asking questions, stumbling, and learning and it was through that openness that they grew strong in faith. No matter our age or experience, there is always more room to grow, more depths to venture into, and more wisdom to discern. Today, choose the humble posture of a learner and make yourself a sponge in the presence of God.

The heart of the prudent getteth knowledge;
and the ear of the wise seeketh knowledge.

PROVERBS 18:15

A difficult crisis can be more readily endured if we retain
the conviction that our existence holds a purpose—a cause
to pursue, a person to love, a goal to achieve.

JOHN C. MAXWELL

Instead of giving people a piece of your mind,
give them a piece of your positive attitude.

POWER UP

When was the last time you humbled yourself to seek guidance, and
how can you cultivate a daily attitude of curiosity and teachability?

_____

_____

_____

_____

_____

THE FLOW OF FAITH

If you can't fight and you can't flee . . . flow.

ROBERT ELIOT

At some point in our lives we find ourselves in situations we can't escape and can't control, and in those moments God invites us to *flow*. Instead of resisting with fear or frustration, we can lean into His presence, trusting that His Spirit will carry us through. Flowing doesn't mean giving up, but releasing the battle into God's hands. When we stop striving and start trusting, we discover His strength lifting us and His wisdom guiding us, even in the places we never thought we could stand. Trust in the One who calms the storms.

Worry does not help anything, but it hurts everything.

GENERAL GEORGE S. PATTON

"Therefore I tell you, do not worry about your life . . . Look at the birds of the air; they do not sow or reap or store away in barns, and yet your heavenly Father feeds them. Are you not much more valuable than they? Can any one of you by worrying add a single hour to your life?"

MATTHEW 6:25-27 NIV

Become a "possibilitarian". No matter how dark things seem to be or actually are, raise your sights and see possibilities—always see them, for they're always there.

NORMAN VINCENT PEALE

POWER UP

Are there unchangeable circumstances in your life that you're struggling against right now, that might serve you better if you chose to flow with them instead?

CALLED TO STRETCH

Unless a man undertakes more than he possibly can do,
he will never do all he can do.

HENRY DRUMMOND

Sometimes the only way to discover the full strength God placed within us is by stretching beyond what feels possible. When we step out in faith and take on challenges that seem bigger than us, we create room for God's power to meet us in our weakness. Playing it safe may keep us comfortable, but it rarely calls forth our best. By daring to aim higher, dream bigger, and lean harder on God, we uncover capacities we never knew we had and realize that with Him, we can do far more than we ever could on our own.

And he said: "Truly I tell you, unless you change and become like little children, you will never enter the kingdom of heaven."

MATTHEW 18:3 NIV

Our attitude at the beginning of a task will affect its outcome more than anything else.

JOHN C. MAXWELL

Coaches who can outline plays on a blackboard are a dime a dozen. The ones who win get inside their players and motivate.

POWER UP

Reflect on a time God gave you strength or practical provision when you were at the end of your rope.

STEPPING STONES
TO SUCCESS

> *The person interested in success has to learn to view*
> *failure as a healthy, inevitable part of the process of*
> *getting to the top.*
>
> DR. JOYCE BROTHERS

Failure is part of the journey for anyone set on getting somewhere in life. While it may sting in the moment, the wise person sees these as lessons that refine our character, sharpen our skills, and draw us closer to the wisdom God wants us to gain. Success is rarely linear — it's built on perseverance, humility, and the courage to rise again after a fall. When we learn to see failures as opportunities, we begin to embrace them as a stepping stones toward the victory God has already prepared for us.

We tend to get what we expect.

NORMAN VINCENT PEALE

No discipline seems pleasant at the time, but painful. Later on, however, it produces a harvest of righteousness and peace for those who have been trained by it.

HEBREWS 12:11

The human spirit is never finished when it is defeated . . . it is finished when it surrenders.

BEN STEIN

POWER UP

How might your journey toward success transform if you began to see each failure as a vital step in shaping you for the road ahead?

THE WORRIES OF YESTERYEAR

It doesn't pay to worry. If you went through last year's files marked "important," chances are the only things you'd keep are the paper clips.

ROBERT ORBEN

Take a moment to think back: what were you most worried about in different seasons of your life? Perhaps when you were a teen, you worried about fitting in with your peers and passing math class, or about your career path and future spouse in your twenties. As we mature mentally and spiritually, what felt so heavy then often loses its weight in the light of the wisdom gained now. Instead of storing up anxieties, invest your trust into the faithful, time-tested source of peace: God. He saw you through yesterday, and He will take care of you today, tomorrow, and every day to come.

*Success is going from failure to failure
without loss of enthusiasm.*

ABRAHAM LINCOLN

*Do not be anxious about anything, but in every situation,
by prayer and petition, with thanksgiving, present your requests to God.*

PHILIPPIANS 4:6 NIV

*My attitude has always been . . . if it's worth playing,
it's worth paying the price to win.*

PAUL "BEAR" BRYANT

POWER UP

*What is something that felt like a huge deal to you at one point in
your life, that you now realize wasn't as important as you thought?*

FAITH IN UNCHARTED WATERS

The man who goes farthest is generally the one who is willing to do and dare. The "sure-thing" boat never gets far from the shore.

DALE CARNEGIE

I t's easy to cling to the safe path, staying close to the shore where the waters feel calm and familiar. But growth and purpose often come when we're willing to step outside of what is familiar and venture into uncharted waters. Life's greatest journeys are not found in comfort zones but in the daring steps of faith that stretch us beyond what we thought possible. Don't let the fear of leaving the harbor hold you back—there are new depths of blessing and understanding where trust and courage meet.

Know ye not that they which run in a race run all,
but one receiveth the prize? So run, that ye may obtain.

1 CORINTHIANS 9:24

Most people are very close to becoming the person
God wants them to be.

JOHN C. MAXWELL

Leadership has less to do with position than it does
with disposition.

POWER UP

Are you wading in the shallows or might God be calling you to
deeper waters?

OPEN EYES, SOFT HEART

J ust as the body can grow stiff without move-
ment, the heart and mind can harden when we
stop dreaming. Somewhere between our teens
and adulthood, many of us lose our capacity for imagination that made childhood magical. "*Psychosclero-
sis*" creeps in quietly with routine, responsibility, and
sophistication. But God calls us to live with childlike
wonder, open to fresh vision and new beginnings. When
we nurture a flexible mindset, we invite God's creativity
to flow through us. Keep your heart soft, your attitude
teachable, and your dreams alive. Life is richest when
you refuse to stop imagining what God can do next.

We cannot hold a torch to light another's path without brightening our own.

BEN SWEETLAND

He is wise in heart, and mighty in strength: who hath hardened himself against him, and hath prospered?

JOB 9:4

Before a person can achieve the kind of life he wants, he must think, act, walk, talk, and conduct himself in all of his affairs as would the person he wishes to become.

ZIG ZIGLAR

POWER UP

Where could your heart use the softening touch of hope and faith?

_____

_____

_____

_____

_____

THE SECRET TO SUCCESS

> *Those folks who succeed simply remain enthusiastic longer than those who fall.*
>
> RALPH WALDO EMERSON

Success often isn't about being the smartest, fastest, or most talented, but being the most persistent. Life's trials can drain our energy, but those who determine to stay actively hopeful and consistent discover that perseverance is the road to victory. When we keep our hearts and minds alive with gratitude and focus, we carry a fire that keeps us moving forward when others give up. God rewards the steadfast, and with His strength, we can keep our zeal burning bright through every season.

We make a living by what we get,
but we make a life by what we give.

WINSTON CHURCHILL

. . . give thanks in all circumstances;
for this is God's will for you in Christ Jesus.

1 THESSALONIANS 5:18 NIV

Winners concentrate on winning;
losers concentrate on getting by.

JOHN C. MAXWELL

POWER UP

What can you do today to rekindle your enthusiasm and keep it
burning long enough to carry you through the challenges ahead?

FACING THE GIANTS

> *Any fact facing us is not as important as our attitude toward it, for that determines our success or failure.*
>
> NORMAN VINCENT PEALE

We all have "facts" we have to face. Perhaps you were born with a health condition that makes life more complicated or you come from a poor or broken home — these facts themselves don't determine our future, but it's the way we respond to them. Take inspiration from the courage of David when he faced Goliath. With God's help, we can choose courage over fear, faith over despair, and gratitude over grumbling. Our attitude, shaped by hope and trust in Jesus, transforms the "giants" in our lives into testimonies.

I have learned to be content whatever the circumstances.

PHILIPPIANS 4:11 NIV

An optimist sees an opportunity in every calamity; a pessimist sees a calamity in every opportunity.

HERBERT V. PROCHNOW

People who never do any more than they get paid for, never get paid for any more than they do.

POWER UP

How can you shift your attitude right now to face today's challenges with faith instead of fear?

CHARACTER IN THE QUIET

We are all guilty of putting on an act when others are watching at some point in our lives, but the true measure of our character is found in the quiet moments when no one sees. Do we still choose kindness when there's no recognition? Do we still live with integrity when no one is keeping score? It is behind the closed doors of our hearts and minds that He both convicts us and shapes us into people of authenticity and strength. When our private life aligns with His truth, our public life naturally shines with grace and influence.

*Attitudes are nothing more than habits of thought . . .
and habits can be acquired.*

PAUL J. MEYER

*Order my steps in thy word:
and let not any iniquity have dominion over me.*

PSALM 119:133

*Our attitude toward life determines life's attitude
toward us.*

JOHN C. MAXWELL

POWER UP

*Left to your own devices, what is the driving force
behind what you think and do?*

THE LIGHT OF HOPE

*Your attitude tells the world
what you can expect from life.*

Our attitude is like a billboard that announces to the world what we believe about life and what we're ready to receive. A heart filled with gratitude attracts opportunities and blessings because it stands out as a hopeful light in a dark world. On the other hand, a negative, bitter outlook shuts doors before they can even open. When we choose to see each day as a gift and carry ourselves with joy, peace, and expectation, we're essentially declaring, *"I believe God has good things in store for me."* And with that posture, we begin to see His promises come alive in our lives.

. . . God is present in the company of the righteous.

PSALM 14:5 NIV

Ability is what you're capable of doing. Motivation determines what you do. Attitude determines how well you do it.

LOU HOLTZ

Nothing can stop the person with the right attitude from pursuing his goal.

POWER UP

What does your attitude testify to those around you?

PERSISTENCE WINS THE BATTLE

> *Ninety percent of all those who fail are not actually defeated . . . they simply quit.*
>
> **PAUL J. MEYER**

Most of our battles in life are not lost because we were defeated, but because we gave up before the breakthrough came. Failure is demoralizing, but scripture reminds us to "*not grow weary in doing good, for at the proper time we will reap a harvest if we do not give up*" (Galatians 6:9). Every step forward, no matter how small, is a step closer to the victory God has prepared for you. Keep pressing on, even when the road feels long, because persistence is often the difference between quitting and conquering.

Start a crusade in your life to be your very best.

WILLIAM DANFORTH

Righteousness keepeth him that is upright in the way: but wickedness overthroweth the sinner.

PROVERBS 13:6

Enthusiasm and persistence can make an average person superior; indifference and lethargy can make a superior person average.

WILLIAM WARD

POWER UP

What goal or dream have you given up on that God might be nudging you to pick up again?

FINISHING STRONG

---

*It's not where you start—
it's where you finish that counts.*

ZIG ZIGLAR

A person sprinting at the beginning of a marathon may be impressive initially, but when you take into account how many miles are ahead, true wisdom is observed in the person conserving their energy with a steady pace. You may feel behind in life, overlooked, or like your past disqualifies you, but God measures success by how faithfully you run your race, not by where you started on the track. Paul wrote, "I press on toward the goal to win the prize for which God has called me heavenward in Christ Jesus" (Philippians 3:14). With God's strength and patience, you can cross that finish line with victory and joy.

. . . "'You have been faithful with a few things; I will put you in charge of many things. Come and share your master's happiness!'"

MATTHEW 25:21 NIV

There is little difference in people, but that little difference makes a big difference. The little difference is attitude. The big difference is whether it is positive or negative.

CLEMENT STONE

*Gratitude is the least of virtues;
but ingratitude the worst of vices.*

POWER UP

*Take a moment to look back at how far you've come.
What answered prayers are you living in today?*

PERSPECTIVE

All looks yellow to the jaundiced eye.

ALEXANDER POPE

Our perspective colors everything we see. A bitter or negative spirit can make every circumstance seem bleak. But when we allow God to heal our hearts and renew our minds, our vision changes. We begin to see His goodness, His blessings, and His hand at work, even in hard places. Proverbs 15:15 reminds us, "*For the despondent, every day brings trouble; for the happy heart, life is a continual feast.*" Choose to let God cleanse your outlook, and you'll find that life looks a whole lot brighter through eyes of faith.

The righteous is more excellent than his neighbour:
but the way of the wicked seduceth them.

PROVERBS 12:26

[It is] tragic when we put off living. We dream of a magical
rose garden over the horizon and miss the roses blooming
outside our windows.

DALE CARNEGIE

Two men looked through prison bars—
one saw mud, the other stars.

POWER UP

What lenses typically color your perspective? Which might you be
better off without or would make a beneficial addition?

STRETCHING TO STRENGTH

> *Do a little more each day*
> *than you think you possibly can.*
>
> **LOWELL THOMAS**

God has given you more strength and potential than you realize, and sometimes the only way to discover it is to stretch just a little further than you think you can. Whether that's taking a step out of your comfort zone to show kindness, being a little more bold with your faith, or taking a baby step forward towards a goal, slow and steady is the key to lasting change. When you do a little bit more each day, you build endurance and open doors you never thought possible. With God's help, the "little more" you give each day will transform your life and the life of those around you.

*Superiority—doing things a little better
than anybody else can do them.*

ORISON SWETT MARDEN

*Cast not away therefore your confidence, which hath great
recompence of reward. For ye have need of patience, that,
after ye have done the will of God, ye might receive the
promise.*

HEBREWS 10:35-36

Attitude determines the altitude of life.

EDWIN LOUIS COLE

POWER UP

What is a step you could take to exercise endurance?

_____

_____

_____

_____

_____

FAITHFUL IN THE SMALL, GREAT IN THE KINGDOM

True greatness consists in being great in little things.

CHARLES SIMMONS

When we ponder greatness, it's usually grandiose exploits, genius inventions, and mighty acts of bravery. One look at the life of Jesus reminds us that it is the small acts that often carry the deepest meaning. Jesus Himself washed the feet of His disciples, a simple act that became a profound display of unimaginable humility and love. When you choose grace in a tense moment, offer kindness in passing, or serve without recognition, you are living out the greatness He calls you to.

*Where there is no vision, the people perish:
but he that keepeth the law, happy is he.*

PROVERBS 29:18

*Since your thinking has a direct bearing on your
performance, your thinking must be based on sound input.*

ZIG ZIGLAR

*We are what we repeatedly do.
Excellence, then, is not an act but a habit.*

POWER UP

*What is a small area of your life in which
you could exercise simple greatness?*

SPIRITUAL STRENGTH TRAINING

> *Chance favors the prepared mind.*
>
> **LOUIS PASTEURA**

Life is full of opportunities that come when we least expect them, but those moments are best embraced by hearts and minds that are ready. Scripture tells us to *"be prepared in season and out of season"* (2 Timothy 4:2), reminding us that preparation is an act of faith and trust in God's timing. When we build up our spiritual muscles through study, prayer, and practicing diligence in times of calm, we position ourselves to step boldly into the missions God sends our way. Chance may look like coincidence, but to the prepared, it becomes a God-given moment to shine.

A wise man will hear, and will increase learning; and a man of understanding shall attain unto wise counsels . . .

PROVERBS 1:5

I don't know what your destiny will be, but one thing I know: the only ones among you who will be really happy are those who will have sought and found how to serve.

ALBERT SCHWEITZER

The only alternative to perseverance is failure.

POWER UP

What spiritual muscle have you trained up well, and what other area could use your attention?

OUR SACRED BEST

> *There is always a best way of doing everything.*
>
> RALPH WALDO EMERSON

God is a God of order and excellence, and He leads us into the "best way" of living, working, and loving others when we seek Him. While the world often tells us to rush or cut corners, Scripture reminds us, *"Whatever you do, work at it with all your heart, as working for the Lord"* (Colossians 3:23). The best way isn't always the easiest or the fastest, but it is the way that honors God and testifies His glory to others. When we invite Him into our daily choices, He shows us how to approach each task with wisdom, grace, and purpose, turning the ordinary into something sacred.

What benefit did you reap at that time from the things you are now ashamed of? Those things result in death! But now that you have been set free from sin and have become slaves of God, the benefit you reap leads to holiness, and the result is eternal life.

ROMANS 6:21-22 NIV

Nothing would be done at all if a man waited until he could do it so well that no one could find fault with it.

CARDINAL NEWMAN

If thinking is viewed as a skill . . . it can be improved by practice, as we improve other skills.

POWER UP

How do you honor and acknowledge God in your living and working?

FAITH RELAYED

L ife is not meant to be a race we run alone but a relay where we build upon the faith of those who came before us. Hebrews 12 gives us a wonderful reminder that we are "*surrounded by a great cloud of witnesses,*" cheering us on as we carry the baton forward. God places people and lessons in our path so we don't have to begin from scratch. Every truth instilled and every act of love laid down before us becomes a foundation for our own growth and calling. Let's take hold of what has been handed to us and run our leg of the race with faith and perseverance.

Then he said to his disciples, "The harvest is plentiful but the workers are few. Ask the Lord of the harvest, therefore, to send out workers into his harvest field."

MATTHEW 9:37 NIV

Anybody who accepts mediocrity—in school, on the job, in life—is a person who compromises, and when the leader compromises, the whole organization compromises.

CHARLES KNIGHT

Behind every great idea is someone saying, "It won't work."

POWER UP

What role model of faith and wisdom helped form the foundation of your life?

IMPULSE VS. PURPOSE

*Great things are not done by impulse
but by a series of small things brought together.*

In life, as in faith, it's rarely the grand moments that shape our destiny, but the small choices we make every day. Each prayer whispered, each act of kindness offered, each moment of perseverance when it would be easier to quit—all of these add up to something far greater than we can see in the moment. God weaves these "small things" into a tapestry of purpose, reminding us that consistency and faithfulness matter far more than flashy beginnings. When we choose to cultivate the right attitude in the little steps, we lay the foundation for great things that will stand the test of time.

I can do small things in a great way.

JAMES FREEMAN CLARKE

But when you are invited, take the lowest place, so that when your host comes, he will say to you, 'Friend, move up to a better place.' Then you will be honored in the presence of all the other guests.

LUKE 14:10 NIV

Progress is not created by contented people.

FRANK TYGER

POWER UP

What small choice could you make today that could have a big impact?

THE BEST YOU HAVE

> *I do the very best I know how—the very best I can; and I mean to keep on doing so until the end.*
>
> ABRAHAM LINCOLN

There's something powerful about the simple resolve to do the best you can, day after day. Through all the seasons of our lives, our best can vary and sometimes seem very little by the world's standards. Here's the truth: God never asked for our perfection, but our devotion. When we commit to giving the best of what we know and have with humble sobriety, we can rest knowing that God multiplies our efforts in ways we may never see. The power of attitude lies in pressing forward with integrity and consistency, trusting that even our smallest "best" offered at the feet of the Lord honors Him and blesses others.

Behold, I send you forth as sheep in the midst of wolves: be ye therefore wise as serpents, and harmless as doves.

MATTHEW 10:16

The great reward for doing is the opportunity to do more.

JONAS SALK

There is no speed limit in the pursuit of excellence.

POWER UP

What is your "best" in this current season of life?

ABOUT THE AUTHOR

J ohn Maxwell is one of the world's most respected authorities on leadership and personal effectiveness. He has written more than a hundred books, including the *New York Times* best seller *The 21 Irrefutable Laws of Leadership*, which has sold more than 4 million copies. In addition to his writing career, he is a popular speaker, inspiring more than 250,000 people annually at appearances nationwide.

Dr. Maxwell's advice is based on his thirty-plus years of experience as a pastoral and organizational leader. He is founder of Maxwell Leadership, an organization that helps people maximize their personal and leadership potential. He has served as a senior pastor for churches in California, Ohio, Indiana, and Florida.

Dr. Maxwell lives in Atlanta, Georgia, with Margaret, his wife of more than fifty years.

Additional copies of this book and other titles
from Honor Books are available online.
Also available from this series:

The Power of Thinking Big
The Power of Leadership
The Power of Attitude
The Power of Influence